Stream of Color

ADVENTURES in Landscape Quilting

Quilters Guide to Landscape Design

JUNE JAEGER
style

Published Courtesy of
Log Cabin Quiltworks

DISCLAIMER

Adventures in Landscape Quilting
©2013 by June Jaeger

Log Cabin Quiltworks
PO Box 496
Prineville, OR 97754

www.logcabinquiltworks.com

No part of this product may be reproduced in any form, unless otherwise stated, in which case reproduction is limited to the use of the purchaser. The written instructions, photographs, designs, projects, and patterns are intended for the personal, noncommercial use of the retail purchaser and are under federal copyright laws; they are not to be reproduced by any electronic, mechanical or other means, including informational storage or retrieval systems, for commercial use. Permission is granted to photocopy patterns for the personal use of the retail purchaser.

Attention teachers: June Jaeger encourages you to use this book for teaching, subject to the restrictions stated above.

The information in this book is presented in good faith, but no warranty is given nor results guaranteed. June Jaeger has no control over choice of materials or procedures, the company assumes no responsibility for the use of this information.

Credits:

Publisher: Log Cabin Quiltworks
Editor: Jean Wells Keenan
Technical Editor: Linda Adams
Technical Layout: Lori Pintok-Snyder
Illustrators: June Jaeger & Lori Pintok-Snyder
Designer: June Jaeger
Photography: Debbie Groshong & June Jaeger
Quilts By: June Jaeger, unless otherwise designated

"Don't waste time waiting for inspiration.

Begin and inspiration will find you."

H. Jackson Brown, Jr.

High Mountain Lake

ACKNOWLEDGEMENT

My appreciation goes to a team of friends who have pitched in to make this book possible. Their support, believing in me, gave me the strength and endurance to pursue this project. A special thank you goes to a great friend, Linda Adams. She has typed, re-typed, proofed and re-proofed the book numerous times. I'm sure she knows it by heart by now.

Thank you to my sister, Jean Wells Keenan, for all of her support, suggestions, and guidance. This book would not have been possible if it wasn't for her encouragement to keep going.

Also, I want to express my sincere appreciation to my Aunt June and Uncle Truxton Ringe for their generosity, love and support.

To all my students, thank you for your encouragement. Because of you, I felt the purpose to write this book. You have been an inspiration to me. Watching your *"light bulb"* come on and seeing you create your beautiful pieces fill my heart and soul. You make it all worthwhile.

I am thankful for the knowledge gained from each and every teacher I have taken a class from. Their input has helped me develop an individual style and to learn the techniques that work well with this style of quilt.

Thank you:
- Jean Wells Keenan
- Karla Alexander
- Charlotte War Anderson
- Ruth McDowell
- Joan Colvern
- Laura Schultz-Smith
- Velda Newman
- Katie Pasquini-Masopust
- Rosalie Dace

DEDICATION

I dedicate this first book to my students who have encouraged me to write and share my ideas, and also to my mother who believed in me.

Metolius River

Table of Contents

Foreward 7

Introduction 8

Inspiration 11

Tools 12

Fabric Choices 14

Pattern Design 16

Preparing the Pattern 18

Tracing Pattern Pieces 21

Fusing to Fabric 22

Placement of Pieces 24

Final Fusing 26

Squaring Up 28

Borders 30

Mitered Corners 32

Abstracting 33

Layering the Quilt 34

Quilting 36

Quilting Exercises 38

Continuous Binding 42

Sleeve for Hanging	44
Quilt Labels	46
Student Gallery	48
More Inspiration	54
Projects	56
Forest	58
Ocean	60
Three Sisters	62
Windmill - High Desert	64
Lake Side	66
Crater Lake	68
Mountain Valley	70
High Mountain Lake	72
Canyon River	74
Waterfall	76
Conclusion	78
Resources	79
About the Author	80

"Creativity is... seeing something that doesn't exist already."

Michele Shea

Foreward

My earliest memories of my sister, June, relate to her drawing of horses. She's a natural artist who has transformed the special things in her life on her quilts.

Spending time together pursuing our art I am amazed at the detail that she sees in something that inspires her, whether it be a shadow beside a tree, or the texture on a rock. She is one of those people who sees possibilities.

Through the years her traditional quilting took more and more of a backseat when she embraced her *"illustration"* talents and started putting them to work in her quilts.

She is a wonderful teacher and truly embraces learning. Her desire for a student's success tops her priorities in the classroom. As you work through the process that June has set out in *"Adventures in Landscape Quilting"* you will find yourself captivated and wanting to design one-of-a-kind quilts.

Enjoy!

Jean Wells Keenan

"The world of reality has its limits; the world of imagination is boundless."

Jean-Jacques Rousseau

INTRODUCTION

The outdoors and nature have always been a big part of my life. Discovering the combination of quilting and nature has prompted me to write *"Adventures in Landscape Quilting"*.

How many times have you visited a place and been totally captivated by it's beauty? We all have our memories of a special place that we would like to capture the essence of. Now you can do it with your own hands. *"Adventures in Landscape Quilting"* will lead you through the steps of designing your own landscape quilt. This book also includes patterns for you to jump-start the process.

You will find a discussion on fabric selection, as well as, complete instructions on using the fusible appliqué technique. A quilt is not a quilt until it is *"quilted"*. Detailed instructions and quilting designs will lead you through the quilting process. Finishing techniques are discussed, giving you different options.

Step-by-step you will create your personal *"place to be"*. From photo to fabric you can bring into existence your very own masterpiece.

"Shoot for the moon, even if you miss it you will land among the stars."

Les Brown

Inspiration may be a form of super consciousness or perhaps subconscious — I wouldn't know. But I am sure it is the antithesis of self-consciousness.

Aaron Copland

Inspiration

Every day when I wake, I see a different sunrise. The sky is constantly changing which changes the color of the foliage on the trees, the reflection on the rocks and the color of the mountains. Every day is different.

It is up to you to become aware of your surroundings and the daily changes. When you are driving to and from work, *(how boring)*, start to notice the color changes on that continuous freeway sound barrier wall. Observe the distant trees changing their seasonal clothes. One day they are lime, another forest, and another they are red. The water draining off the hill, pooling along the side of the road, reflecting the sunset, what an inspiration. These are quilts in the making. Look at the irrigated field with the blue sky reflecting off the water next to the deep green row crops, the ice cycles hanging from a roof, and the reflection of a prism in rainbow colors. Yes, these are the simple things of life that carry hidden beauty.

We all can be intrigued by huge waterfalls, magnificent mountains and the Grand Canyon, but in our own backyard we can find instant beauty. We just need to look and allow ourselves the moment to enjoy that view. You will learn to see things differently and appreciate it to the fullest.

Your favorite place, a memorable trip, your home growing up, your own backyard can all be recreated in your next quilt. Take a photo, draw a sketch, and remember. This is your chance to bring to life memories through fabric and art.

Dream... Achieve

Tools

For Landscape Design

Good Acrylic Gridded Rulers

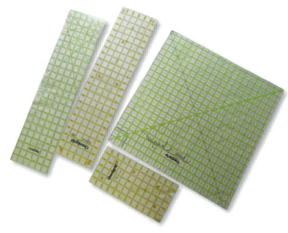

These rulers work well for squaring up the quilt. I love the 20 ½" by 20 ½" square and the 6" by 24" ruler, which I also use to cut my borders. Add another ruler of any size when squaring up the landscape.

Large Cutting Mat

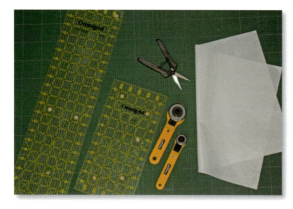

Bigger is better, but you can slide your project around on a smaller mat. Most generally I use a 24" by 35" mat for squaring up the landscape and for cutting borders.

Rotary Cutter

Use a medium size rotary cutter for borders and squaring up. For cutting landscape pieces that are less intricate, you can use a very small rotary cutter.

Sharp Pointed Scissors

A small scissor with very sharp points can get into those little curves. I prefer the small Fiskars™ scissors that are spring loaded.

Colored Pencils

Color code pattern pieces using colored pencils.

Teflon™ Pressing Sheet

This has become a favorite tool. Use it to protect your iron and pressing surface. Also, use this sheet for assembling sections. You can use parchment paper in place of the Teflon™ sheet.

Light Box

To assemble pattern pieces, place pattern on the light box, then the Teflon™ sheet. The lines will show through the sheet for placement.

Blue Painters Tape

Taping the pattern and pressing sheet together, keep it from slipping.

Zip Lock Bags

You don't want to lose any of the cut pattern pieces. Store these pieces in plastic bags. Use one bag per fabric. Usually sandwich bags are large enough, but sometimes the one or two gallon size bags are necessary for the larger pieces.

Sewing Machine

Use a sewing machine that you are familiar with, and in good working order. Sew borders on with the machine and quilt with it, dropping the feed dogs. A good straight stitch machine will work. A walking foot and a darning foot are needed.

Pencils & Pens

You will need a #2 pencil for drawing and a fine point Sharpie™ pen for tracing.

Pins

I prefer the flat quilting pins for stabilizing and the 1" safety pins when layering my quilt for quilting.

Thread

There are many different threads to choose from for quilting, depending on the texture you want. Isacord™ and Aurifil™ are good all around threads. YLI™, Superior™, King Tut™, and Sulky™ are my favorite variegated threads. Superior Thread™ has put out a thread designed for the bobbin called *"The Bottom Thread"*. It works great, or you can use the top thread in the bobbin.

Helpful Hint

GREAT STUDENT IDEA

You can make your own portable light box using a large shallow transparent plastic storage tote. My box is 14" X 20" and 5" deep. Turn the box upside down and place an under-the-counter light strip under the box. BiMart, KMart or any multi-purpose store will have the supplies. When not in use, you can store your supplies in the box.

Fabric Choices

Fabric choices can be a tricky business. When choosing fabrics for a landscape you will find yourself studying the photo. You will see things you have never noticed before.

Water can be baffling because of it's reflections. Notice how it will mirror image an object, but the reflection is distorted. Wind and current will cause this, so you are seeing more than a body of water, you are seeing movement. Adding a touch of white can make water look rough and angry, or it can be a reflection of a cloud, or a mountain. Dark at the edge of water gives the impression of shade or high banks. In kindergarten we learned water is blue. Notice, that isn't always true.

A snow scene can be unsettling because of so much white. By adding a touch of light lavender and light blue, they give the snow dimension and take out the flatness. A light shade of gray helps to create shadows in the snow.

Foliage isn't just green. It is a multiple of greens, olives, limes, tans, browns, reds, taupes, and golds. Depending on seasons you will see more of one color than another. By your choice of fabric, you can change the season. Not only will you notice color, but you will also notice value changes, lights and darks.

Variety is the key here. When picking fabrics, look at texture as well as the color. Batiks are what I prefer. They are a tighter weave of fabric, higher thread count, so there is less fraying. The colors are truly rich and vivid on both the front and the back.

I see rock fabric, tree fabric, water, but they are not pictures of rocks, trees, or water. They are texture. Use your imagination to see them as the subject you want them to be. Try to view batik fabric as sky, fields, brush, rivers and rocks, but really it is just pretty textured fabric, which is perfect for landscape. Batiks have a handmade look which is not repetitive.

This is the time when you can get creative personalizing your picture using fabric. Choose more fabrics than what you will use; it will give you more options. If you select a high contrast fabric it will draw your eye to that fabric. Use it sparingly, and in at least three different places. If you use it only once it will look like a bullseye.

The question of preshrinking fabrics always comes up. If making a wall quilt preshrinking isn't necessary. The reason is when fabric comes off the bolt it has a finish on it that preserves the color. The high quality of fabric today eliminates the concern to preshrink.

If making a bed quilt, lap quilt or baby quilt then preshrink because these will be laundered.

"Art is satisfying your sense of surprise."

Pattern Design

Eliminate the Unnecessary Details. *Start Simple!*

Once you work out the idea of the technique then start adding more difficult patterns and add challenges. It is like putting together a puzzle; start with the basics, then get more pieces, more challenging fabrics, and designs.

Using the overhead projector to design patterns is an easy way for the less confident artist to draw their pattern. Start with a photo of a landscape. Place a piece of transparency film that you can write on over your picture, with a fine point Sharpie™ trace the lines. Anytime there is a color change this will be a line. Each line must connect either to itself or another line, thus making the shape an island. Each island represents a different piece of fabric. Eliminate small details. Let your fabric do the work for you.

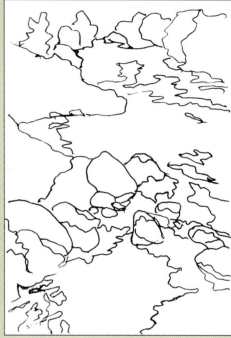

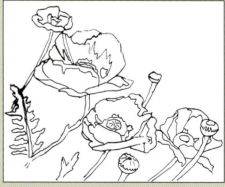

Take the transparency to the overhead projector placing it face side down. This will reverse the traced image onto the wall. With masking tape or blue painter's tape attach a piece of butcher paper, the size of the proposed design, to the wall. Turn on the overhead projector. You will find the image enlarges when you move the projector away from the wall. If you move it closer to the wall the image will get smaller. Once you have obtained your desired size use the side knob to fine tune the clarity of the lines.

On to the butcher paper, trace all the lines using a #2 pencil. Do not use a Sharpie™ at this point as it will bleed through onto your wall. Turn the projector off to make sure you have traced every line before you remove your drawing. Turn it back on to trace any missed lines. Place your picture next to your drawing, it should be a mirror image of your pattern.

Take your newly drawn pattern to a table. Place a piece of plastic or paper under your drawing so the pen does not come through on the table. Using a Sharpie™ pen trace all the pencil lines.

If you are using a black and white enlargement from an office supply center, follow the steps below.

Once you have the enlargement, draw your lines directly on the enlargement using a Sharpie™ to designate your islands. Then use the back side for your reversal or trace the lines onto a piece of tracing paper or on clear vinyl. This will become your pattern. (You can purchase clear vinyl at any hardware store.) You will be using the reverse side of your enlargement to trace your pattern pieces.

Be careful not to use someone else's photo without written permission.

Helpful Hint

If you do not have an overhead projector you can enlarge your photo by going to an office supply store or printing shop. I prefer to have my photo enlarged in black and white so I can readily see the value changes in the picture. Have the store use the cheaper paper.

Preparing Your Pattern

Using colored pencils, color each shape with a pencil that will represent it's particular fabric. Every fabric change has to have a colored pencil change.

For example, if there are three green trees, all different greens, color each tree with a different green. Each of these greens will represent three different green fabrics.

As shapes are colored, make fabric selections. Cut a small swatch from each fabric to represent that colored pencil. To make a legend on a corner of your pattern, tape the fabric swatches on one side of your legend and color a square with the representing colored pencils next to that swatch. It makes it a whole lot easier to designate fabrics ahead of time.

To help you identify the placement of your pieces, assign a number to each pattern piece. When assigning numbers I work from the top to the bottom in numerical order so that the sky has the smallest number and the foreground at the bottom has the largest number. This will help with the placement of pieces.

Now that the pattern is ready for tracing, double check the fabric choices you have made. Lay the fabrics in the order they are listed on the legend. Place the photo next to the fabrics and determine if you are satisfied. If not, it is easy to make changes in fabric now.

Tracing Pattern Pieces

Wow, now you can start tracing!

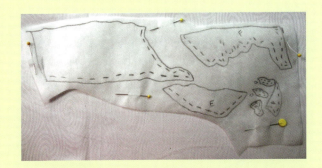

Using a light fusible web of choice, trace around each individual island (pattern piece). Fusible web comes with a paper side and a glue side. Place the fusible web paper side up over the pattern. Trace on the paper side of the fusible web with a #2 pencil or a Sharpie™ pen. When tracing leave at least ½" of space around each island.

The bottom of each piece will need to have an overlap allowance of about ⅛". Draw a dotted line to indicate where the overlap is located on each piece (see example). Looking at your pattern from top to bottom you will notice the shapes become nearer to you as you get closer to the bottom. Each island will need to fit underneath the next piece down as you are working toward the foreground. The over lap allowance makes this possible so the base fabric does not show through. Check off each island on your pattern when you trace it. This will avoid tracing a piece twice.

When drawing rocks study them and determine what rock is in front of what rock. The rock that is the furthest behind will be the first rock placed. It will have an overlap allowance added to the sides where the next rock will sit on top of it, and so on. The last rock to be placed will have no allowance added as it is the closest rock to you. The earth below will overlap the rock formation so there needs to be an allowance added at the bottom of the rock to tuck nicely under the ground.

This applies to trees as well.

Make sure you read the directions on the fusible web that you have chosen. Each fusible has different time and iron temperature instructions.

Fusing to Fabric

Cut around the pattern pieces. **Do not cut on the drawing lines.** Lay the fabrics out. Place each piece with it's designated fabric. Take the fabric and it's pattern pieces to the iron. Place the fabric **wrong side up**. Lay each pattern piece onto your fabric with the

drawing side up. Lay a Teflon™ pressing sheet on top. With the iron press two to four seconds (check fusible web manufacturer's instructions). If using steam, cover the pattern pieces with a pressing cloth. Allow it to cool. Repeat with each fabric and it's designated pieces. If a piece has not stuck to the fabric check the temperature of the iron and repeat with a two second press.

Helpful Hint

Green Scrubby can be used for removing fusible web that is stuck on your Teflon™ pressing sheet.

Mt. Hood

Helpful Hint

After cutting out your fabric pieces, notice they are the reverse of your pattern drawing. When you start placing your pieces this will make sense.

Cut out the islands (pattern pieces) along the drawing lines, except where you need to overlap pieces, then cut on the overlap allowance lines. Store these pieces in ziplock bags, each fabric to it's own bag.

Use the negative part of the fabric for additional shapes to fill in more color.

Placement of Pieces

A base fabric is needed to fuse the pieces on to. Most generally I use the sky fabric as a base. Cut this base two inches larger, both in length and width, of the proposed landscape.

To begin, lay all the pieces within the area you are working, next to your light box. Then place the original drawing face-side down on the light box. To make your own light box see *"Great Student Idea"* on the Tools, page 13. Place a Teflon™ sheet over the pattern drawing, using blue painter's tape attach them together. Concentrating on a small section of the pattern you will assemble a group of islands to form a bigger island. If I were doing a mountain scene, I would start with one mountain, assembling all the pieces of that mountain, and set it aside. Then assemble another mountain and set it aside.

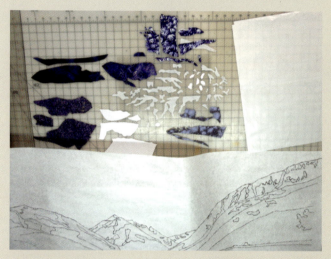

Remove the paper from the back of the pattern piece. To take the paper off the back of the fused fabric bend a corner toward the paper side and the fold separates the paper from the fabric. Remove slowly making sure the fusible stays with the fabric.

Begin a section with the piece with the lowest number. Place it on the Teflon™ sheet, sticky side down matching it to the drawing lines. Take the second piece and remove its paper. Place it overlapping the first piece matching its drawing lines. Most generally you will be working from top to bottom numerically.

When a section is completed tack the islands together with the iron for two seconds. Allow to cool before removing the section from the Teflon™ sheet. To remove the section from the Teflon™ sheet start at one corner and slowly roll the Teflon™ away from the island. Do not place this assembled island on paper; it will stick to the paper. Place it on a piece of parchment paper or plastic. Continue, repeating with small sections.

When working with small pieces you can place those on top of their island, such as snow on a mountain.

Once you have the small sections completed **lay the base fabric** over the pattern taping or pinning it to the pattern. Still working on the light box, starting with the sky (base fabric), place the top section onto the base, lining it up to the pattern drawing. Working from the background to the foreground place the islands, ending with the piece that has the highest number and is the closest image to you. This piece most generally is at the bottom of the picture.

Three Sisters with Juniper

Final Fusing

Once all of the sections have been placed set the original photo next to the landscape. Double check to make sure you have not left a piece out, also recheck the placement. At this point you can still change things if you are not satisfied.

Lay the landscape out on a large flat ironing surface. Check the manufacturer's directions for the time for the final fusing. Add steam if directed, or use a dry iron, if specified. If using steam, use a pressing cloth rather than a Teflon™ pressing sheet to protect your iron. Place this over the landscape and press with the iron in a lower and lift motion, usually ten seconds. Do not slide the iron. Let cool before moving the landscape.

"Creativity is harnessing universality and making it flow through your eyes."

Peter Koestenbaum

Helpful Hint

DRYER SHEETS - *If you happen to get fusible web stuck on the iron use a dryer sheet. Put the hot iron on the sheet and rub the iron across it until the glue is removed.*

"I paint not by sight but by faith, Faith gives you sight."

Amos Ferguson

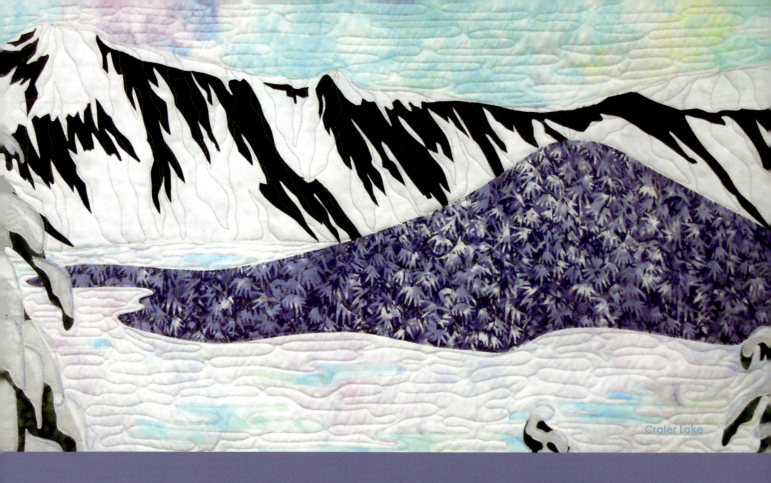

Crater Lake

Squaring Up

Not everyone has a large gridded cutting mat to use for squaring up so I like to use rulers. I use a large square gridded ruler 20 ½" by 20 ½" along with a 6" by 24" gridded ruler and any other 6" gridded ruler.

Lay the large square ruler on top of the project at one corner, butt the 6" by 24" ruler to one side of the square ruler, letting it extend down one side. The other 6" ruler is butted across the top edge at a 90 degree angle. Visually, check a horizontal line, making sure the rulers are straight. If not, twist the rulers one way or the other until they appear straight.

Using a rotary cutter, cut the excess fabric from the outer edge of the side and off the top edge. Now the top and one side are squared up.

Move the square ruler to the other top corner, lining it up on the trimmed edge. Butt the 6" by 24" ruler to the square ruler on the untrimmed side. At this point I like to check the side to side measurement of the picture, using a tape measure. Trim off the outside excess on this side.

Move the large square ruler to the bottom corner. Lay the 6" by 24" ruler across the bottom, butting it up to the large square. Using a tape measure, check the top to bottom measurement, making sure you are staying square. Trim the bottom edge.

Borders

Borders are not mandatory but they do frame a quilted picture well. It gives a matted look when a narrow inner border is added, with a wider outer border.

When choosing borders, try interviewing the fabrics by placing them next to the quilt. You want the picture to be the main focus. You never want it to compete with a border that is too busy or too strong. The border is there to enhance the picture and to frame it. It should allow your eye to focus on the lines and colors within the picture. Using a very dark fabric for the narrow inner border gives your picture a visual stopping point.

To splice a border because the fabric is not long enough, splice on a diagonal. The diagonal line will allow your eye to flow off of it, while a straight line splice will draw attention to itself.

Cut the border widths first. Then place one strip face-side up onto the sewing machine with the tail off to the left. Then place the next strip face-side down onto the first strip with the tail falling into your lap. Where they overlap each other forms a square. Sew a diagonal line from the top left corner to the bottom right corner.

Trim seam to ¼". Press open. You now have a long even border strip.

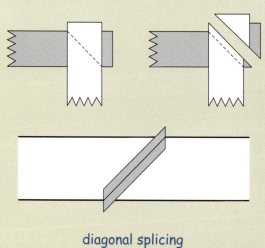

diagonal splicing

Cut the first border 1 ¼" wide by the length of the top and bottom measurement of the picture. Pin both ends and one in the middle. Sew these borders (¼" seam) to the top and to the bottom of the quilt. Press out.

Measure your picture sides. Cut the side borders 1 ¼" by this measurement. Pin. Sew to the sides of the picture. Press out.

The width of your outside border will be dependent on the size of your quilt. Use a size that is visually pleasing to the project. A 4" border works well on medium to large wall hangings. Measure the picture, cut your top and bottom pieces. Sew. Press. Repeat the steps for your side borders.

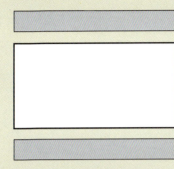

add side borders

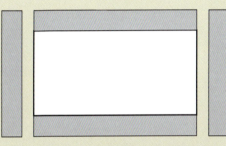

add top and bottom borders

finished with borders

"Satisfaction of one's curiosity is one of the greatest sources of happiness in life."

Linus Pauling

Mitered Corners

Another option is to do mitered corners. For mitering, the border strips must extend beyond the quilt the width of the border plus a few inches on each side.

Pin the top border, right sides together to the quilt, centering the top border so you have overhang on both ends. Start stitching ¼" in from the edge of the quilt top, back tack, then sew to the other edge, stopping ¼" from the edge, back tack. Press the seam toward the border. Repeat for the bottom border.

Pin one side border, centering, leaving overhang on both ends. Start your stitching ¼" from the edge of the quilt, back tack. Sew down the side, stopping ¼" from the end, back tack. Press toward the border. Repeat with the other side border.

With the right side of the quilt up, press the top border out flat. Lay the side border on top, mitering the corner at a 45 degree angle as shown. Press the corner. Pin the borders together. (See diagrams)

Fold the quilt diagonally so the right sides of the top and side borders are together. Pull all seam allowances out of the way. Sew on the pressing line. Do not sew over the other seams. Trim seam allowances to ¼". Press open.

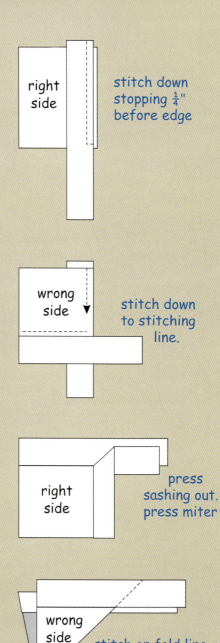

Abstracting

The Crossing

To mute or abstract the background so that the foreground becomes the focus, you can cut fabrics into small pieces.

To accomplish this, fuse the backs of a few different fabrics, cut them apart in strips and cross cut them making random shapes and sizes. Then start picking and choosing pieces and placing the background. It is kind of fun to not follow a set pattern. Making puzzle pieces come together is creative and self-satisfying. Every so often stand back and assess the process, making the changes if needed. Do not final fuse until you are satisfied with your placement.

For further abstraction, a good reference book is *"Intuitive Color & Design"* by Jean Wells, C&T Publishing.

"During periods of relaxation after concentrated intellectual activity, the intuitive mind seems to take over and can produce the sudden clarifying insight which gives so much joy and delight."

Fritj of Copra, physicist

ABSTRACTING 33

Layering the Quilt

Cut the backing and batting four inches larger than the finished top. Lay the backing fabric face-side down on a large flat surface. Stretching the fabric slightly, tape each corner to a flat surface. Tape in between the corners. You want the backing to be tight with no wrinkles.

Place the batting on top of the backing, smoothing out from the center to the outside edges. You will find the batting sticks to the backing.

Lay quilt top on the batting, face side up. From the center, smooth the top out to the outside edges.

Using quilter's safety pins, start pinning the quilt in the center. Pin every four to six inches, working your way out to the borders and the outer edges. Snap the pins closed after you have placed the last pin.

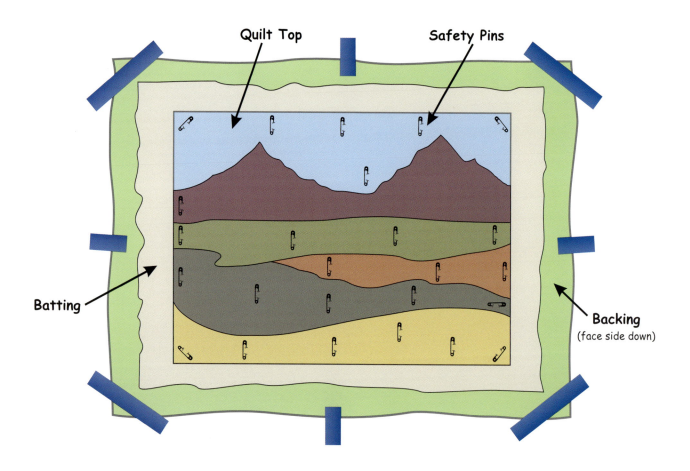

"To become truly immortal, a work of art must escape all human limits: logic and common sense will only interfere... once these barriers are broken, it will enter the realms of childhood visions and dreams."

Giorgio De Chirico

Quilting

Quilting by Betty Ann Guatalupe

I prefer to machine quilt landscape quilts on my domestic machine. You are sewing through multiple layers and many are batik fabrics with a high thread count, making it difficult to hand quilt. Machine quilting is an art that takes practice.

Often times you cannot find thread to match the fabric, so you can use a gray. Keep on hand a light, medium and dark gray. You will use two different feet on the machine to accomplish two different tasks, both a walking foot and a darning foot.

To stabilizing the quilt use a walking foot for straight line quilting. The feed dogs are up with this foot. Stitch around each border in the *"ditch"*. The stitches are on the side of the seam that you have pressed away from, so you are stitching next to the side which has the bulk of the seam allowance.

Next, remove the walking foot from the machine and put on the darning foot. Drop the feed dogs; you may have to refer to your sewing machine manual to accomplish this. You are now ready to freehand quilt. Because the feed dogs are dropped you have all the control in your hands. Start by pulling the bobbin thread to the top. Hold the thread securely and take three very tight stitches. Begin moving your hands, controlling the quilt to move where you want to stitch. The stitches should be about 14 stitches to the inch. To end, again, take three very tight stitches and trim off the threads.

Top stitching and quilting are done in the same step. Section off the quilt and stitch to further stabilize the project. I quilt on the outer edge of each mountain, hill, lake and tree line first. Then go back and fill in each section with more detailed quilting. See exercises for quilting lines.

Helpful Hint

Quilting Gloves - *You can substitute gardening gloves that have the little rubber dots.*

Three Sisters

Quilting Exercises

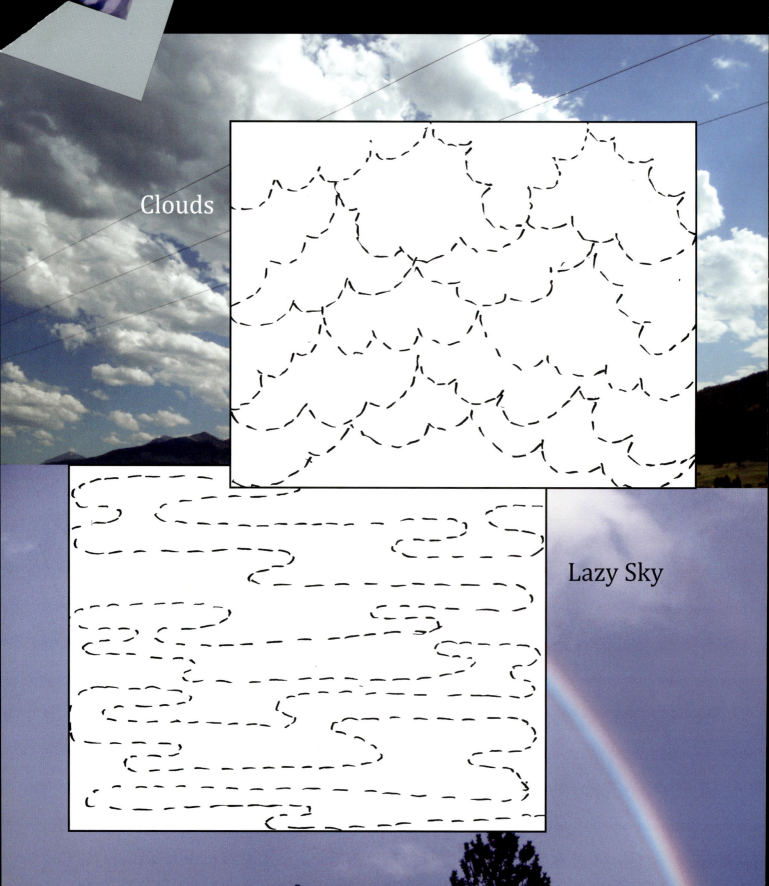

Clouds

Lazy Sky

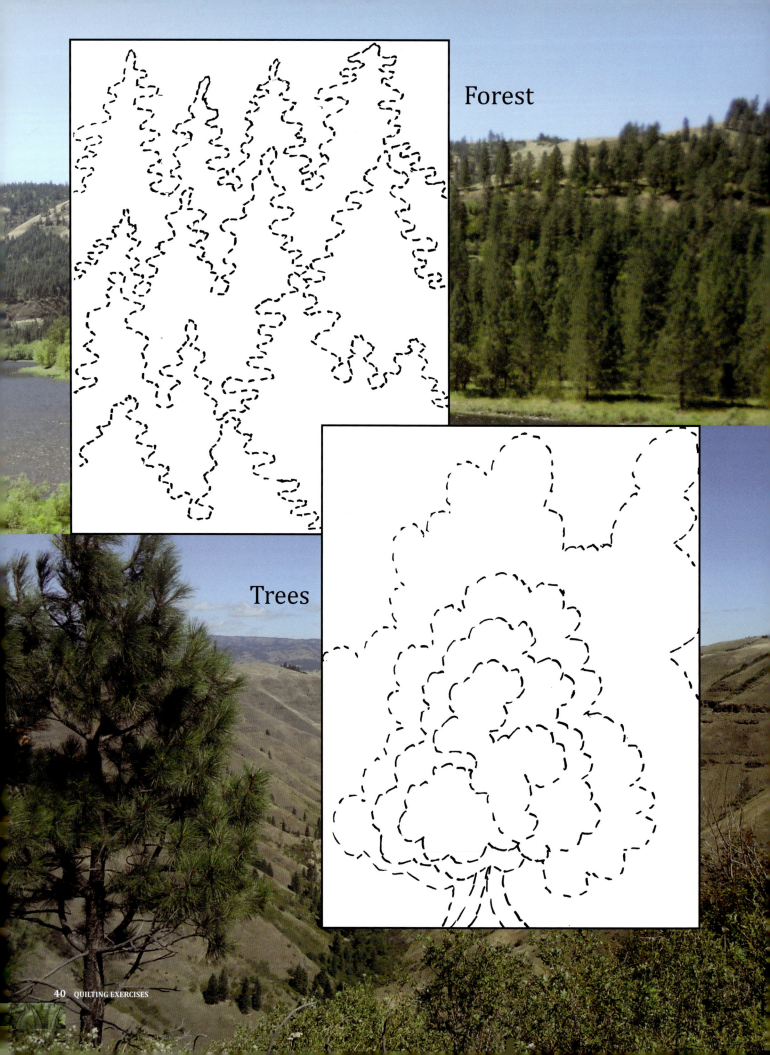

Continuous Binding

Cut the binding strips on the straight of grain of the fabric. Cut the strips 2 ½" wide by the length or width of the fabric, which ever is the longest. Splice on the diagonal. Refer to the splicing instructions in the *"Borders"* section. Press in half lengthwise with the right side out.

Use a walking foot when attaching the binding. Begin about one third of the way up one side of the quilt. Place the binding with the fold in toward the center of the quilt. Align the raw edges with the edge of the quilt top. Using a ¼" seam start stitching in about ten inches from the end of the binding. Stop and back tack ¼" from the first corner. Clip the threads and turn the quilt so you can work on the next side.

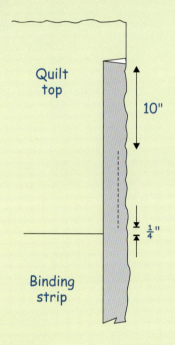

Fold the binding up, creating a 45 degree angle, and then fold back down, even with the second side of the quilt. This forms a little pleat. Start stitching at the outer edge of the fold, as shown.

Continue stitching to the next corner, repeat the turn, fold and stitch the third and fourth sides. Stop about ten inches from the point of beginning. Remove the quilt from the sewing machine.

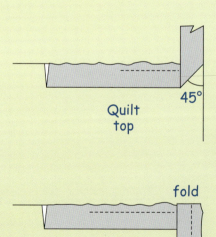

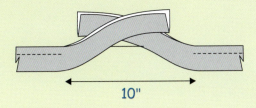

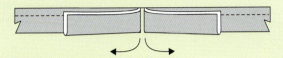

Fold back the beginning and ending tails of the binding so they meet in the center of the unsewn portion. Press the folded edges.

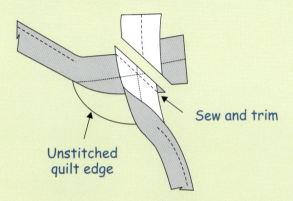

Unfold both edges of the binding and match the center points of the two folds, forming an X as shown. Pin and sew the two ends together on the diagonal of the fold lines. Trim the excess binding tails ¼" from the seam. Press the seam open. Refold the binding and finish sewing to the quilt.

Fold the binding over the edge of the quilt to the back. Hand stitch the binding in place, covering the machine stitching line. Hand stitch the mitered corners.

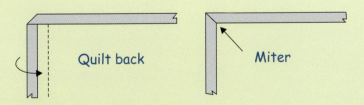

Sleeve For Hanging

It is preferable to construct a sleeve for all of wall hangings. They will hang straight across with no drooping. Most quilt shows require a 4" wide finished sleeve.

Measure the quilt width. Your sleeve will be finished 1" narrower than the quilt.

If you are putting a binding on your quilt, I recommend tying the sleeve in with the binding. After you have stitched your binding on, but before you turn the binding to the back, stitch the sleeve in place, sewing over the binding stitches.

Cut a fabric that matches the backing 9" wide by the width of the quilt. Press both ends in toward the back ½". Stitch them in place. Fold the fabric in half lengthwise. Press the fold. Pin the sleeve on the top back of your quilt, matching raw edges, centering the sleeve. With the binding laying flat against the quilt (out of the way) stitch directly on the ¼" seam which you used to sew on your binding.

Making a pleat up to the raw edges, press this narrow pleat in place. Repress the bottom of the sleeve giving it a new fold line. Pin the bottom of the sleeve on this fold line. Hand stitch this fold to the back of your quilt. The pleat allows extra fabric for the hanging rod.

Fold the binding to the back of the quilt covering the raw edges of the quilt and pocket. Stitch in place.

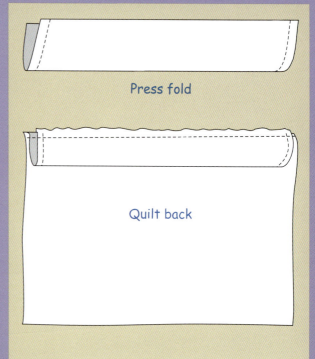

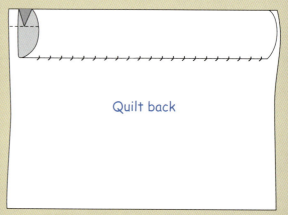

If you are not putting on a binding, it is easier to make a finished pocket and hand stitch it in place.

Cut the fabric for this sleeve 9" wide by the width of the quilt. Fold in each end ½", press and sew. Place the right sides together lengthwise and stitch ¼" from the edge. Turn right sides out. Press this tube. Press a fold ¼" from the top of the sleeve. Pin the sleeve to the back of the quilt ¼" from the top. Hand stitch the sleeve to the quilt on the sleeve edge, allowing this fold to create a pleat at the top of your quilt. Fold this pleat up, pin the bottom of your sleeve to the back of your quilt. Hand stitch in place.

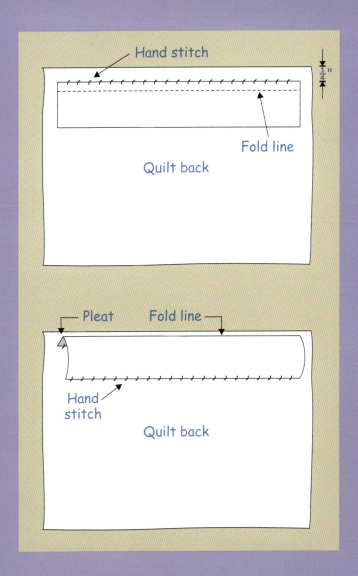

"Look and you will find it – what is unsought will go undetected."

Sophocles

Quilt Labels

How many times have you come across a quilt and wondered when it was made, who made it, and where did it come from? Many quilts from the 1800's were considered utilitarian quilts; they had a purpose. This is true of the 1920's and 30's also; very seldom have we seen any verbiage on these quilts. If only quilts could talk, we would know a lot more about our history. Quilt historians can give us general information, but can not tell the quilt's story.

Documenting your quilt with a label on the back answers those questions. Labels don't have to be fancy, just informative. They need to tell us the name of the quilt, who made it, who quilted it, where the maker lived at the time, and the year the quilt was made. It is that simple. The label is your signature.

You can add for whom the quilt was made. If it was a special project, you can add the purpose for making the quilt, such as a donation, or a gift. Honoring a holiday can be documented. There are a number of reasons for making a quilt; add this to the label.

"Creative work is play. It is free speculation using the materials of one's chosen form."

Stephen Nachmanovitch

"A painting is never finished —it simply stops in interesting places."

Paul Gardner

Making a label can be as simple as writing with a permanent pen on a piece of muslin, and fusing the label to the back bottom corner of the quilt. Or you can roll the edges under and hand appliqué the label in place. You could also buttonhole stitch around the label.

You could take the theme of the quilt to another level by using it on the label. Making a mountain scene quilt, draw an outline of a mountain on a piece of fusible web, fuse it to the back of a light colored fabric, cut out the mountain image, and write the necessary information, using a fine point Sharpie™ pen. Peel the paper off the back of the image and place the label on the bottom right corner of the back side of the quilt. Fuse into place. The hot iron also heat-sets the ink on the label.

On the *"Stream of Color"* quilt the poppies stood out. I took that theme and drew a poppy on fusible web, fused it to the back of the fabric, and wrote the label information with the permanent pen and fused to the back of the quilt.

Student Gallery

I am honored that these students submitted quilts for the book. Featuring them and their interpretation of their favorite place fills my heart. I watched the struggles, the excitement, and the *"light bulbs"* coming on in each student. As a teacher, this is the most fulfilling moment I can experience. The heart of every student is reflected within their quilt.

For some of these students this was a first quilt, some a first finished quilt, and others a total satisfaction. Good job!

Thank you, students.

Cyprus Point
Candice Spencer
Prineville, OR

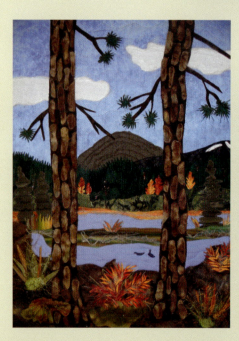
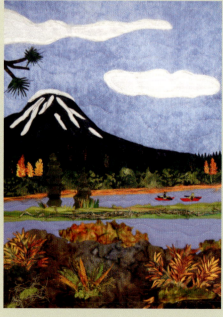
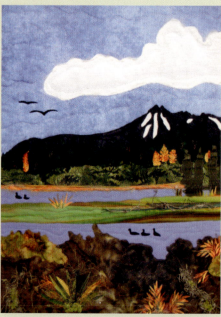

Sparks Lake in Autumn
Kathy Chism, Bend, OR

My Own Backyard
Marney Close
Prineville, OR

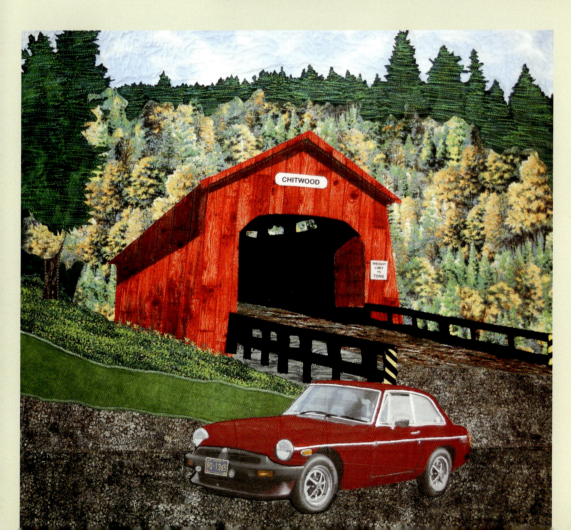

Sunday Drive
Paula Fox
Tualatin, OR

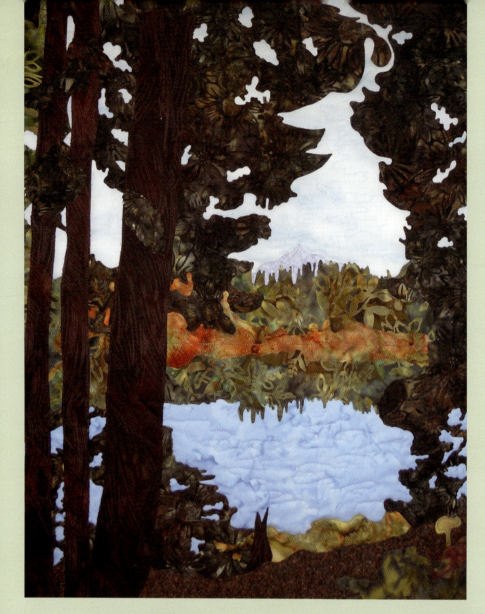

Fall at Clear Lake
Pattie Scheel
Prineville, OR

Keukenhof Gardens of Lisse, Holland
Pennie Patterson, Redmond, OR

Mt. Hood
Christie Crutz, Vancouver, WA

Mountain Creek
Trine Benson
Sisters, OR

STUDENT GALLERY 51

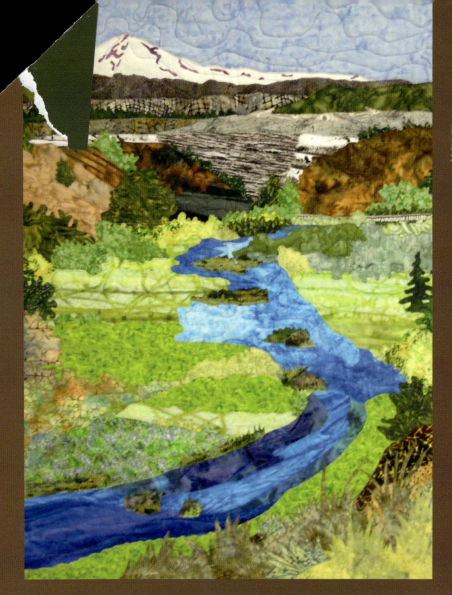

Lower Bridge Road
Judy Beaver
Sisters, OR

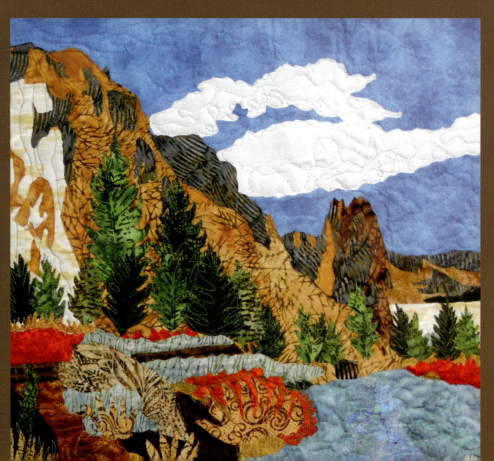

Smith Rock State Park
Elizabeth Leeberg
Bend, OR

Saguaro at Apache Lake
Regina Kelly
San Tan, AZ

Aspens
Terry Thode
Sisters, OR

More Inspiration

This quilt was designed by June Jaeger for the famous Sister's Outdoor Quilt Show in 2011. Every year there is a raffle quilt to help fund the Quilt Show and Kiwanis of Sisters. It was an honor to be chosen as the designer. Pattern is available at the Stitchin' Post in Sisters, Oregon. www.stitchnpost.com

This was a great chance to put together a collection of scenes from the Northwest into one quilt. Keeping the images small, and working on one image a week the quilt was not overwhelming. This is a great example of a theme quilt that anyone could create. This pattern is available at the Stitchin' Post in Sisters, Oregon. www.stitchinpost.com

Projects

These projects have been designed to get you started in the fusible appliqué techniques. They range from easy to more advanced. The amount of fabric needed for each project depends upon the size you enlarge the picture. Once the pattern is enlarged, measure the approximate size of the pieces; document how much you will need of each fabric. First go through your fabric stash and pull what you can use. Then, shop for the fill-ins.

GENERAL INSTRUCTIONS FOR ALL THE FOLLOWING PROJECTS

For detailed step-by-step directions refer to previous chapters: *"Preparing the Pattern"* through *"Final Fusing"*.

1. Enlarge the pattern to the desired size. You have permission to enlarge or reduce these ten patterns. Feel free to change any pattern to suit you. You may want to eliminate a tree or a ground line, or add something special.

2. The pattern has been numbered for your convenience. Use the numbers to correspond with the order of placement of the pattern pieces. Always begin with #1, the sky. It will be your base.

3. Color code the pieces using colored pencils on your pattern.

4. Cut the sky or background base first. Use this block as the base to which you will place and fuse all of the pieces.

5. Trace the pattern pieces onto the paper side of the fusible web. The pattern has been reversed for your convenience. Leave at least ¼" space around each pattern piece. Allow extra space for overlapping pieces.

6. Fuse the pattern pieces to the back side of the appropriate fabrics.

7. Cut out the images (pieces) on the drawing lines, except where they need to overlap. Allow an overlap allowance of ⅛".

8. Remove the paper from the back of the fused pieces.

9. Using the base fabric place all of the pieces, starting with the lowest number, progressing to the highest number.

10. Fuse in place. Please refer to the manufacturer's instructions for time, heat, and if steam is required.

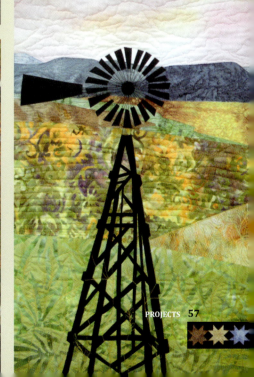

PROJECTS 57

Forest

"Adventures don't begin until you get into the forest. That first step is an act of faith."

Mickey Hart

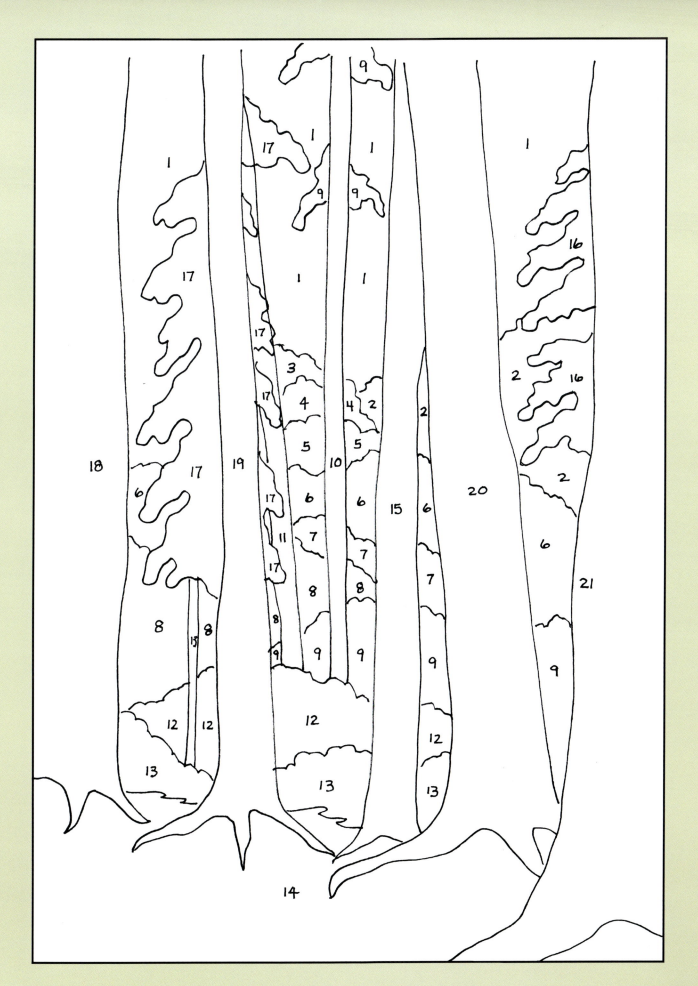

Ocean

"For me a painting is like a story which stimulates the imagination and draws the mind into a place filled with expectations, excitement, wonder and pleasure."

J.P. Hughston

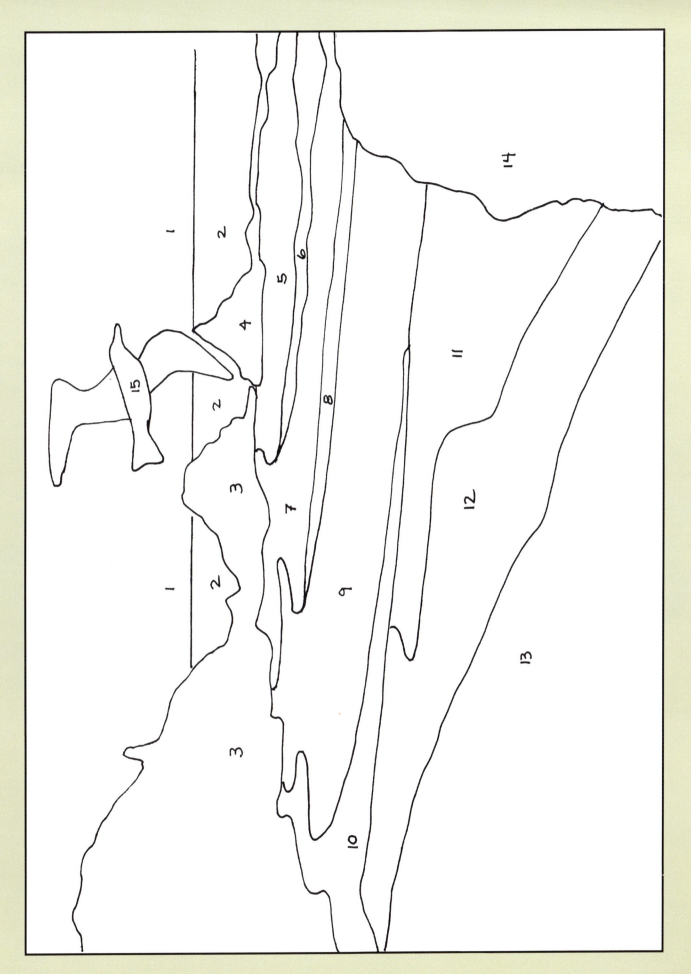

Three Sisters

Place all the small mountain pieces on the mountains, tack before you place onto your sky.

"...our creative work is actually our creativity itself at play in the field of time. At the heart of this play is the mystery of joy."

Julia Cameron

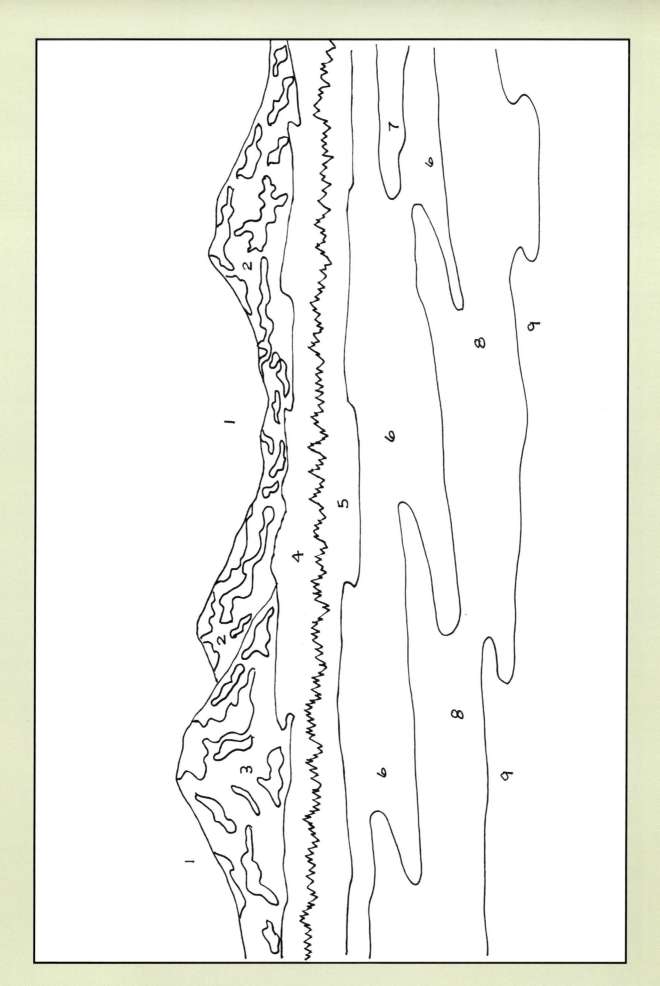

Windmill - High Desert

The windmill blades are uneven on purpose. You want the viewer to realize that each blade is placed individually. Dotted lines are quilting lines. You can construct the understructure of the windmill all as one, rather than separate parts.

"Creation is only the projection into form of that which already exists."

Shrimad Bhagavatam

PROJECTS 65

Lakeside

"No amount of skillful invention can replace the essential elements of imagination."

Edward Hopper

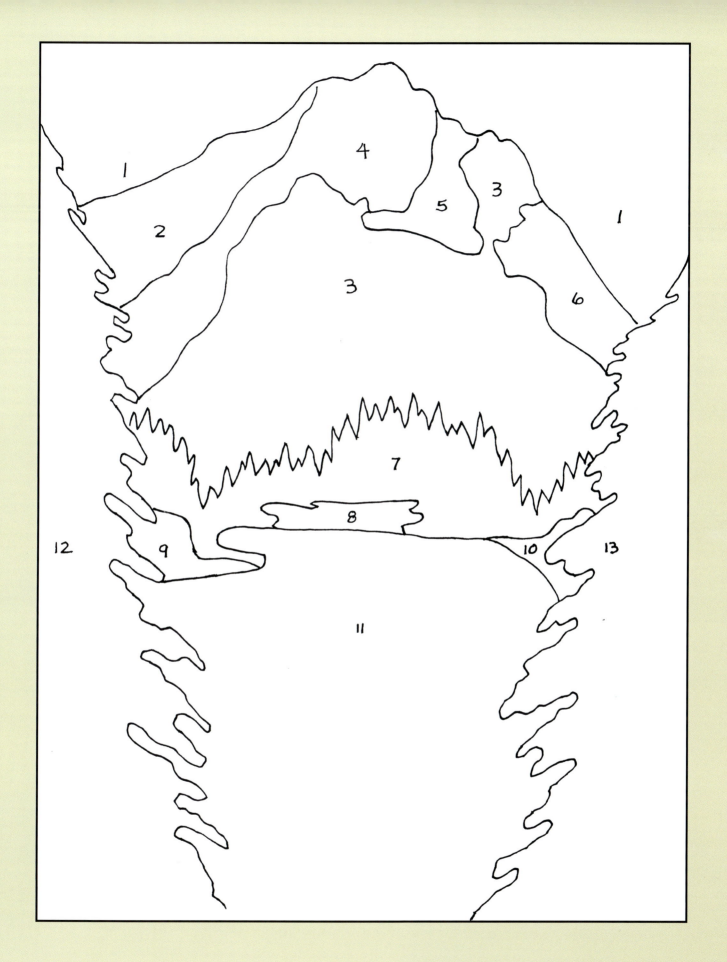

PROJECTS 67

Crater Lake

Assemble trees then place them onto your picture.

"Art evokes the mystery without which the world would not exist."

Rene' Francois-Ghislain Magritte

ain Valley

...ng on the mountain add all of the small dark pieces to the white mountain before placing it. ... cutting the line of trees, you can use the discarded (or reversed) portion for another row of ... at way, you are cutting only once.

"The job of the artist is always to deepen the mystery."

Francis Bacon

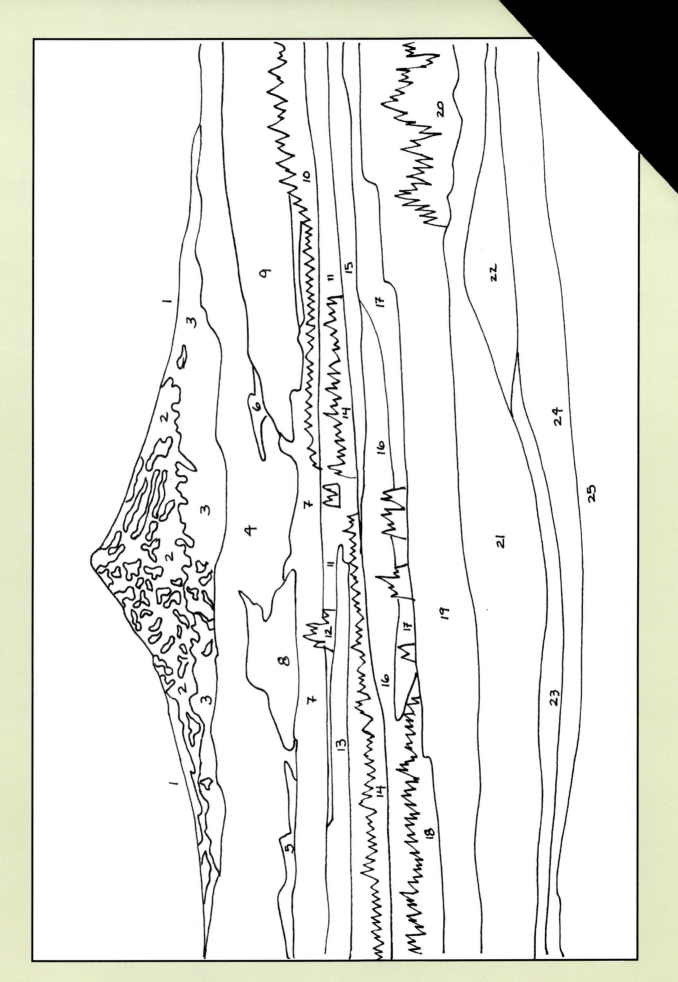

ntain Lake

ns, add the snow and color changes to each mountain before placing that

"The most beautiful thing we can experience is the mysterious."

Albert Einstein

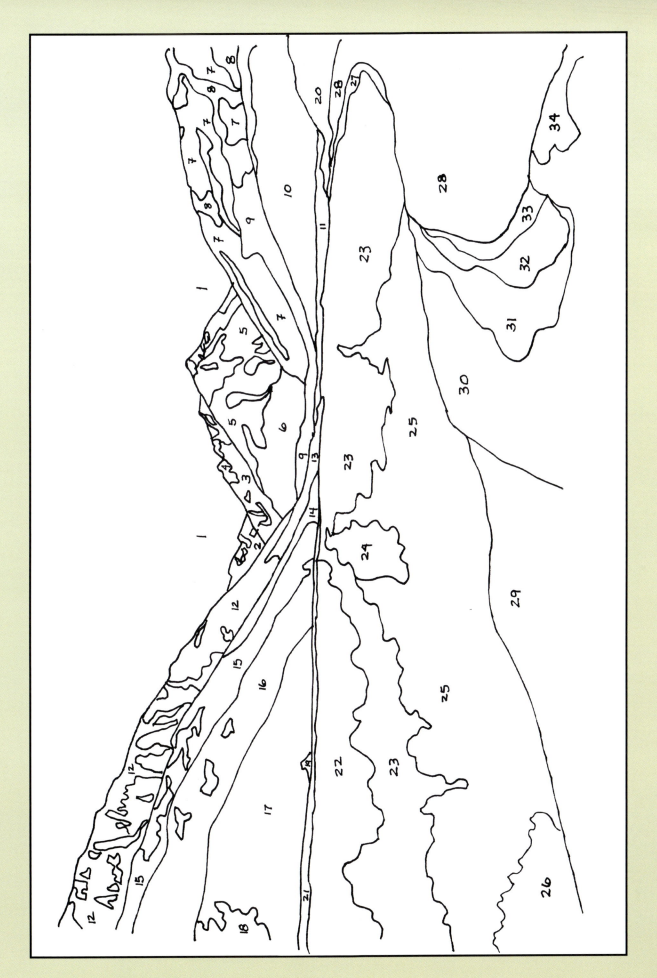

PROJECTS 73

Canyon River

"A painting is never finished... it simply stops in interesting places."

Paul Gardner

Waterfall

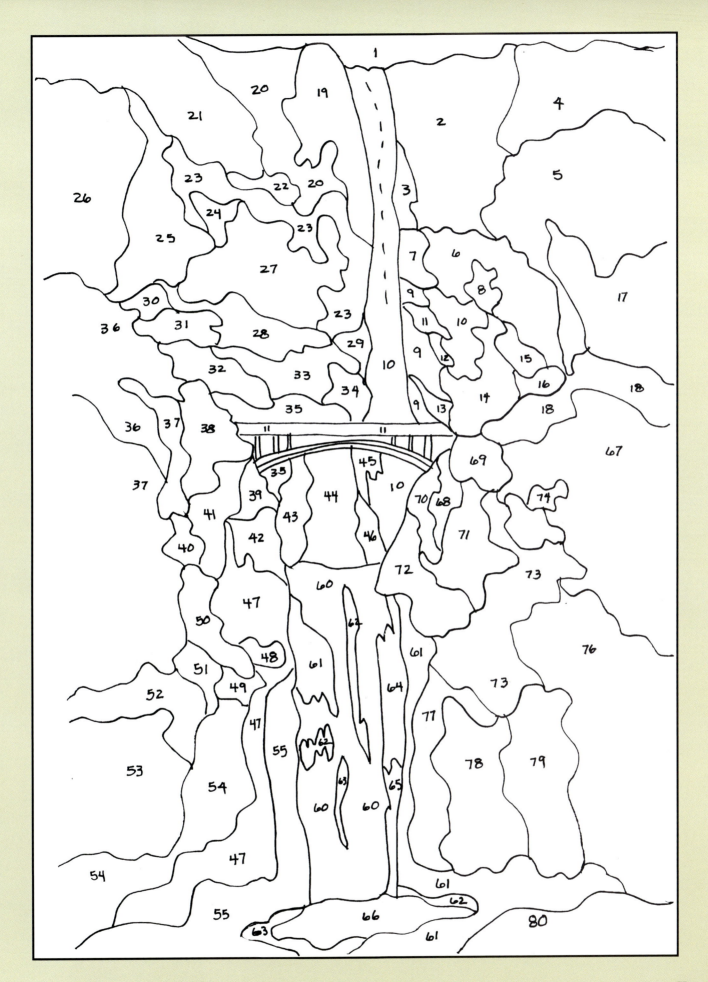

PROJECTS 77

Conclusion

"Adventures in Landscape Quilting" has given you the tools to create your interpretation of a special scene. You will find that each project becomes easier, even though the details become more advanced. Using the step-by-step process, you will become comfortable and excited to start your next landscape. Through your eyes, you will view scenes in a creative manner, noting for a future project.

In conclusion, you are the artist. You have the knowledge, and you have *"Adventures in Landscape Quilting"* as a reference.

Contact information:
June Jaeger
horsinaround@logcabinquiltworks.com
www.logcabinquiltworks.com

Resources

The following are some of my favorite books:

Alexander, Karla – *Stacking a New Deck*, Martingale and Co., Woodinville, Wa.
   (Great use of color in the quilts)

Hargrave, Hariette – *Heirloom Quilting*, C & T Publishing, Lafayette, Ca.
   (One of the first good machine quilting books)

McDowell, Ruth – *McDowell's Piecing Workshop*, and *Design Workshop*, C & T Publishing, Lafayette, Ca.
   (Ruth took design to a new level)

Newman, Velda – *A Painter's Approach to Quilt Design*, Fiber Studio Press, Bothell, Wa.
   (Beautiful painted quilts)

Pasquini-Masopust, Katie – *Fractured Landscape*, C & T Publishing, Lafayette, Ca.
   (A great approach to a different designing technique)

Wells, Jean – *Intuitive Color and Design*, and *Journey to Inspired Art Quilting*, C & T Publishing, Lafayette, Ca.
   (Inspirational color, composition and design books)

Quilting Supply Center:
The Stitchin' Post
P.O. Box 280
Sisters, Oregon 97759
541-549-6061
www.stitchinpost.com

Products:
Lite Steam-a-Seam™
Warm Company
5529 186th Place SW
Lynnwood, Wa 98037
(800) 234-9276

Log Cabin Quiltworks
Pattern Designs
PO Box 496 • Prineville, OR 97754
541-447-2591
horsinaround@logcabinquiltworks.com
www.logcabinquiltworks.com

About the Author

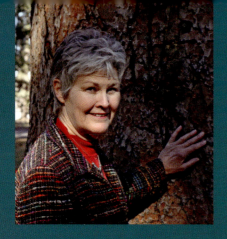

Art has always been a big part of my life. Majoring in Art Education, I focused on oil painting, but enjoyed sketching, water color, charcoal drawing and more. After marrying a rancher I went to work on our place. Running tractors, herding cattle, and training horses became my way of life. Winters were long and depressing, keeping me indoors much of the time. In 1969, my sister, Jean Wells Keenan understood the situation and suggested I make a quilt. By 1980, I was teaching quilting and beginning to add designing to my craft. I quickly became obsessed. I learned I could not only quilt, I was drawing my own patterns, plus I found that I could market them.

A door opened when Daisy Kingdom of Portland, Oregon offered me a job. Teaching and learning the business end of quilt shop ownership intrigued me. In 1993 I opened a quilt shop in Pendleton, Oregon by the name of *"Log Cabin Quiltworks"*. Then in 1998 I moved to Central Oregon where I continued using my store name, but was using it as the business name, for my patterns. Being able to draw and quilt are very important to me, but it also was important for me to fuel my inspiration. I always have a camera and a sketch pad with me whether I am on a pack trip, or hiking or biking. By 2000 I had designed over 75 patterns for various companies. I feature wildlife, nature, horses, and cat patterns.

Many of my quilts have been published in numerous books and magazines. I have been featured in *"For the Love of Quilting"* by Fons and Porter, Back Country Magazine, Ladies Home Journal, and more.

My quilts have been featured at Houston International Quilt Show, Paducah International Quilt Show, Santa Clara International Quilt Show, Mid Atlantic Quilt Fest, Northwest Quilting Expo, and Pacific West Quilt Show. They have won prizes from Best of Show, Judges Choice, First Place, Second Place and Honorable Mention.

I teach throughout the nation, but mainly in the western United States. One of my favorite teaching engagements is the Sisters Outdoor Quilt Show and Quilters Affair, where I have taught for over 30 years. Recently, in addition to doing landscape appliqué, I have started adding painting and inking to my projects. I am always excited about learning new aspects of the quilting world.

Designing and teaching are my priorities, but I still take time to enter an art or quilt show now and then; and always save time to enjoy the outdoors. Life is good!

> *"Every child is an artist. The problem is how to remain an artist once he (she) grows up."*
>
> **Pablo Picasso**